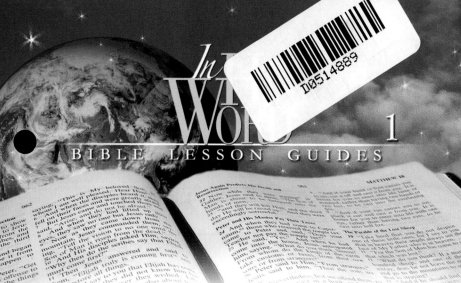

Is There Anything We Can Trust?

Someone recently observed that everything once fastened down has come loose. Never in the history of this country have so many people been so completely confused and disillusioned as they are today. There doesn't seem to be anyone or anything you can trust.

Daily reports of dishonesty, lying, cheating, and willful law-breaking have left the average American stunned and shocked. A number of prominent leaders in the political and social world have been forced to resign their positions or have been sentenced to prison because of the dishonest way they have lived. Large companies have collapsed because of the dishonesty of their officers. Religious leaders have failed to live up to the standard of morality and honesty that they have proclaimed.

A spirit of pessimism and cynicism is sweeping the world. It especially affects young people. But there is good news for everyone. There is something you can believe in, and there is someone you can trust! These are not just idle claims. There is abundant evidence to support them.

There is a book in the world that you can trust: that book is the Bible. The term *Bible* simply means "The Book." It contains 66 different books, or sections, written by 40 authors over a period of 1,600 years (1500 B.C. to A.D. 100). The men who wrote the books of the Bible differed widely in education, occupation, and cultural and intellectual perception. They wrote under differing circumstances on three different continents and one island. Yet in theme and purpose, the Bible is a single book. It speaks of one God; it reveals one Saviour; it uplifts one standard of righteousness.

There is one central message in both the New and Old Testaments. This is because one author inspired all of the men who contributed to the writing of the Bible. That Author is the One who can be trusted, for He is God!

1. **Through what means did the message of truth come to the prophets? 2 Peter 1:21 (KJV 1787; NKJV 1166)**

_____

NOTE: The God of all wisdom spoke through the Holy Spirit to the prophets, who wrote down God's messages and thoughts in their words. This accounts for the variety of ways in which the same thing is said in the Bible. Divine thought in human words makes up the Bible.

2. **How much of the Bible is inspired? 2 Timothy 3:16 (KJV 1750; NKJV 1144)**

_____

NOTE: The Bible is God's message of love and truth to His earthbound children. This is His way of making known to us what His plan and will is for our lives. But some will ask, "How can I know that it is His word and that it can be trusted?"

3. What ability does God claim that sets Him above and apart from all of the other gods that man has worshiped? Isaiah 46:9, 10 (KJV 1081; NKJV 703)

"Declaring _____

_____ done."

Someone has said that prophecy is but history in advance. In the Bible we have many fulfilled prophecies that can be explained only by admitting that God's foreknowledge was responsible for these predictions that have been fulfilled with such amazing accuracy.

The predictions found in the Bible concerning Babylon, Tyre, the Edomites, Jerusalem, Greece, and Rome all demonstrate that this book was divinely inspired by a God who could see the future.

Archaeology has shown the Bible to be accurate in its many historical statements. Dr. William F. Albright says: "Thanks to modern research we now recognize its [the Bible's] substantial historicity. The narratives of the patriarchs, of Moses and the Exodus, of the conquest of Canaan, of the Judges, the monarchy, exile and restoration, have all been confirmed and illustrated to an extent that I should have thought impossible forty years ago."

Contrary to what many have heard, the Dead Sea Scrolls, sealed in pots and hidden in caves to preserve them from the Romans in A.D. 68, when compared with tenth-century manuscripts, revealed no significant differences. "Archaeology has thrown light on the validity of most facts of the Scriptures, so that the believer can say with confidence that while 'the grass withereth' and the 'flower fadeth,' 'the word of our God shall stand for ever' (Isaiah 40:8)."

You can trust the Bible! Jesus did, and His life was guided by the truth that He claimed existed in that book. When tempted by Satan in the wilderness, Jesus was quick to meet the temptation with: "It is written, Man shall not live by bread alone, but by every word that proceedeth out of the mouth of God"—Matthew 4:4. (KJV 1400; NKJV 937)

4. To what three general divisions of the Old Testament did Jesus refer in His teachings? Luke 24:44, 45 (KJV 1544; NKJV 1024)

_____

_____

NOTE: "The law of Moses" was a common Jewish term for the first five books of the Old Testament. "The prophets" include Isaiah, Daniel, Jeremiah, Ezekiel, Joshua, Judges, and the twelve Minor Prophets, plus Samuel and Kings. "The psalms" include all the remaining books.

5. About whom does the Old Testament speak? John 5:39 (KJV 1556; NKJV 1030); Luke 24:25-27 (KJV 1544; NKJV 1024)

_____

6. Why did John say that the experiences of Jesus were recorded? John 20:31 (KJV 1587; NKJV 1050)

_____

7. Why are the experiences of the Bible characters recorded? 1 Corinthians 10:11 (KJV 1680; NKJV 1105)

_____

NOTE: Today we would say "as examples," or "for our counsel." At another time Paul changed the wording slightly when he said, "For whatsoever things were written aforetime were written for our learning, that we through patience and comfort of the scriptures might have hope"—Romans 15:4. (KJV 1666; NKJV 1096). God expected that through a study of the events of the Bible we might be better able to understand His love and His manner of dealing with human beings.

8. **What will the study of the Scriptures do for us?**
   2 Timothy 3:15 (KJV 1750; NKJV 1144)

   _____

   NOTE: When sin broke the direct personal channel of
   communication between God and man, it was necessary for God
   to make known to man His plan, laid before the world began, by
   which He would save man from sin and death. The spoken word of
   God and His written Word were now the means that God would
   use to guide His creatures into an understanding of the way of
   salvation.

9. **For what is all Scripture profitable? 2 Timothy 3:16, 17 (KJV
   1750; NKJV 1144)**

   _____

   NOTE: Doctrine means "teaching, facts, truth." You will notice
   that this text says that it will teach us doctrine. This is just another
   way of saying that God will teach us His truth through this means.
   He will reprove, correct, and instruct us in righteousness that we
   might be able to live the good life that He has planned for each of
   us.

10. **Where did Jesus say we could find the truth? John 17:17 (KJV
    1581; NKJV 1046)**

    _____

An earthly mind sees only a wilderness.
A spiritual mind sees living streams.

NOTE: Mankind does not know what the truth is, and most of the human race do not know how to tell the truth or share it. That is why there are so many problems and heartaches and so few answers to man's dilemma. We are told, "And ye shall know the truth, and the truth shall make you free"—John 8:32. (KJV 1563; NKJV 1035) Truth makes us free from sin and all of the problems and suffering that have come into the world through rebellion.

11. **Why did Jesus say the Sadducees were in error and didn't know the truth? Matthew 22:29 (KJV 1436; NKJV 958)**

_____

12. **Why can't the natural man understand the Bible? 1 Corinthians 2:12-14 (KJV 1671; NKJV 1100)**

"Spiritual things are _____ discerned."

NOTE: "The mind that is earthly finds no pleasure in contemplating the word of God; but for the mind renewed by the Holy Spirit, divine beauty and celestial light shine from the sacred page. That which to the earthly mind was a desolate wilderness, to the spiritual mind becomes a land of living streams"—The Ministry of Healing, p. 460.

13. **Whom did Jesus say would guide us into all truth? John 16:13 (KJV 1579; NKJV 1044)**

_____

NOTE: It is only as the Spirit leads us in the study of the Bible, interpreting to us what He inspired the writers to put down for us, that we will know the truth of God's plans for our lives.

14. **What did the apostle tell us that we should do with the Bible? 2 Timothy 2:15 (KJV 1748; NKJV 1144)**

_____

NOTE: This text does not say we are to just read the Bible. It tells us to study! It requires earnest effort and time on our part if we are to understand the deep things of the Word of God.

15. Why were the Bereans commended? Acts 17:11
    (KJV 1623; NKJV 1071)

    _____

NOTE: They studied daily to see if what they were hearing was right or wrong. What a revolution would take place in the religious world today if those who attend the various churches of the land would begin to study the Bible to see if what is being taught in their church is according to the Scriptures.

    _____

➡ ➡ ➡

Lesson Review

1. God communicated directly with the prophets to get His message through to mankind. ❏ True ❏ False

2. What are the three divisions of the Old Testament to which Jesus referred as He taught?

   a. _____

   b. _____

   c. _____

3. Stories of people in the Bible were recorded so that we can learn from them. ❏ True ❏ False

16. To what does the Bible compare the help we will receive from a study of the Bible? Psalm 119:105; Psalms 119:11 (KJV 946; NKJV 587)

_____

Think It Through

Describe the one thing in your life in which you have the most confidence.

How does being able to have confidence in something make you feel?

- -

4. For what is all scripture profitable?

_____

5. Who should we allow to guide us into truth? (Circle one)

Pastor or priest.

The Holy Spirit.

Our own mind.

Name:_____

Address:_____

City:_____ State:_____ Zip:_____

Contents

1. The Divine Commission 4
2. Your Testimony 7
3. Witnessing About Christ 10
4. What Is the Most Effective Witnessing We Can Do? 15
5. Write Out Your Testimony 19
6. Winning Their Confidence 21
7. Christ—the Center and Theme of All We Do 29
8. How the Work Will Be Finished 35
9. A Simple Method of Giving Bible Studies 37
10. Salvation in the Present Tense 42
11. Helpful Suggestions for Various Situations 45
12. How to Succeed in Giving Bible Studies 53
13. How to Get People Into Bible Studies 57
14. Working for Missing and Inactive Members 62
15. Missing or Inactive Member Survey 69
16. Follow-up of Interests Created by Mass Media 71
17. Principles for Gaining Decisions 74
18. The Science of Securing Decisions 78
19. Using Texts As Direct Personal Appeals 81
20. Discovering Obstacles and Meeting Objections 86
21. Christ's Method of Witnessing and Training 94

The Divine Commission

*"You shall be witnesses to me . . . to the
ends of the earth."*
—Acts 1:8, NKJV.

*"Go ye into all the world, and preach the
gospel to every creature."*
—Mark 16:15.

*"The commission given to the disciples is
given also to us. Today, as then, a crucified
and risen Savior is to be uplifted before
those who are without God and
without hope in the world."*
—Gospel Workers, p. 29.

➤ How are we to accomplish this mission?

1. "How can the great work of the third angel's message
   be accomplished? It must be largely accomplished by
   persevering, individual effort, by visiting the people in
   their homes."—*Welfare Ministry,* p. 97.

2. "This house-to-house labor, searching for souls, hunting
   for the lost sheep, is the most essential work that can be
   done."—*Evangelism,* p. 431.

3. "It is not preaching that is the most important; it is house-
   to-house work."—*Gospel Workers,* p. 468.

4. "For years I have been shown that house-to-house labor is
   the work that will make the preaching of the Word a
   success."—*Evangelism,* p. 433.

5. "Wherever a church is established, all the members should engage actively in missionary work. They should visit every family in the neighborhood, and know their spiritual condition."—*Christian Service,* p. 12.

6. "This work cannot be done by proxy. Money lent or given will not accomplish it. By visiting the people, talking, praying, sympathizing with them, you will win hearts." —*Testimonies,* vol. 9, p. 41.

➤ Every member is to be active

1. "There is not one inactive in heaven, and no one will enter the mansions of bliss who has failed to show love for Christ, who has put forth no efforts for the salvation of others."—*Testimonies to Ministers,* p. 20.

2. "The living church of God will be waiting, watching, and working. None are to stand in a neutral position. All are to represent Christ in active, earnest effort to save perishing souls."—*Testimonies to Ministers,* p. 163.

➤ Every member is to be trained

1. "Every member of the church should be instructed in a regular system of labor. All are required to do something for the Lord. They may interest persons to read; they may converse and pray with them. The minister who shall educate, discipline, and lead an army of efficient workers will have glorious conquests here, and a rich reward awaits him when, around the great white throne, he shall meet those saved through his influence."—*Testimonies,* vol. 5, p. 308.

"There should be no delay in this well-planned effort to educate the church members."—*Testimonies,* vol. 9, p. 119.

2. "Let ministers teach church members that in order to grow in spirituality, they must carry the burden that the Lord has laid upon them—the burden of leading souls into the truth. Those who are not fulfilling their responsibility should be visited, prayed with, labored for."—*Christian Service,* pp. 69, 70.

   "The best help that ministers can give the members of our churches is not sermonizing, but planning work for them. Give each one something to do for others. Let all be taught how to work."—*Testimonies,* vol. 9, p. 82.

3. "That which is needed now for the upbuilding of our churches is the nice work of wise laborers to discern and develop talent in the church—talent that can be educated for the Master's use. There should be well-organized plans for the employment of workers to go into all our churches, large and small, to instruct the members how to labor for the upbuilding of the church, and also for unbelievers. It is training, education, that is needed. Those who labor in visiting the churches should give the brethren and sisters instruction in practical methods of doing missionary work."—*Testimonies,* vol. 9, p. 117.

4. "In every church the members should be so trained that they will devote time to the winning of souls to Christ. How can it be said of the church, 'Ye are the light of the world,' unless the members of the church are actually imparting light? Let those who have charge of the flock of Christ awake to their duty, and set many souls to work." —*Testimonies,* vol. 6, p. 436.

Your Testimony

*"That which will be most effective is the
testimony of our own experience."*
—The Desire of Ages, p. 347.

*"The first works of the church were seen
when the believers sought out friends, relatives, and acquaintances, and with hearts
overflowing with love, told the story of what
Jesus was to them, and what they were to
Jesus."*—Testimonies to Ministers, p. 168.

*"What you need is a living experience in the
things of God, and simplicity in presenting
the love of Christ to the lost."*
—Sons and Daughters of God, p. 266.

➤ Assurance in Christ

Many sincere Christians have been turned off by a person brag-
ging that he is saved. Such people have turned many away from
Christ. On the other side of the coin, many have been puzzled
that some of us who profess to know and love Jesus Christ seem
so timid in talking about Him.

With respect to witnessing, you will notice that we have re-
phrased the old question, "Are you saved?" We now ask a person
if he has the assurance of eternal life.

Paul was positive in talking about his salvation. "I have fought
the good fight," he said. "I have finished the race, I have kept the
faith. Now there is in store for me the crown of righteousness."
—2 Timothy 4:6-8.

Paul says he knows that he will have that crown of righteousness. He does not say that he hopes, or that he thinks—but that he *knows!*

Peter was certain of the future for himself and the believers. In 1 Peter 1:3-5, Peter said he knew that the inheritance was reserved for him.

John knew that he and his fellow believers had eternal life. (See I John 5:11-13.) This letter was written to assure the believers that they had eternal life.

They could believe this, because Jesus had promised eternal life to every believer (see John 6:40, 47). Christ said that He would give everyone who accepted him the gift of eternal life and that He would raise him or her up in the resurrection.

All Christians should have the assurance of four great facts in their spiritual lives, as listed below:

1. **That their sins are forgiven.** 1 John 1:9. Jesus promised to forgive and cleanse us from all unrighteousness. Hebrews 8:12.

2. **That they have been born again.** John 3:3-5. If you have accepted Christ as your Savior, He, through the Holy Spirit, has created you as a new person. 2 Cor. 5:17.

3. **That they have received the Holy Spirit into their lives.** (See John 16:6, 7, 13, 14, and John 3:3-5.)

   a. It is the Holy Spirit who brings us the knowledge of truth, directs us to salvation, and brings about the new birth in our lives.

   b. Don't let charismatics put you to flight. Show them that you know how the Holy Spirit has been active in your life to help you in the ways Jesus said He would.

4. **That they have the assurance of eternal life through Jesus Christ.** Romans 7:24, 25; 1 John 5:11-13; John 6:47.

These references show that these people knew that their sins had been forgiven and that they had salvation. (See *The Desire of Ages,* pp. 331, 338.)

The moment of salvation comes when a person receives Christ into his or her heart through the Holy Spirit.

"'Truly, I say unto you, He that believes in Me has everlasting life.' Through the beloved John, who listened to these words, the Holy Spirit declared to the churches, 'This is the record, that God has given to us eternal life, and this life is in His Son. He that has the Son has life.' 1 John 5:11, 12. And Jesus said, 'I will raise him up at the last day.' Christ became one flesh with us, in order that we might become one spirit with Him. It is by virtue of this union that we are to come forth from the grave, not only through the power of Christ, but because, through faith, His life has become ours. Those who see Christ in His true character, and receive Him into their hearts, have eternal life. It is through the Spirit that Christ dwells in us; and the Spirit of God, received into the heart by faith, is the beginning of the life eternal." —*The Desire of Ages,* p. 388.

Witnessing About Christ

*The disciples shared Christ from
experience with Him.*

➤ They shared their own experience

"Let us gather together that which our own experience has revealed to us of the preciousness of Christ, and present it to others as a precious gem that sparkles and shines. Thus will the sinner be attracted to Him."—*Review and Herald,* March 19, 1895.

➤ What is God's desire for us?

"God desires that the receivers of His grace shall be witnesses to its power. . . . He desires that His servants bear testimony to the fact that through His grace they may possess Christlikeness of character . . .

"His blessings He presents in the most alluring terms. He is not content merely to announce these blessings; He presents them in the most attractive way, to excite a desire to possess them. So His servants are to present the riches of the glory of the unspeakable Gift."—*The Desire of Ages,* p. 826.

➤ What is a witness?

Webster's dictionary defines a witness as "one who has personal knowledge of something."

A witness is simply one who . . .
• Tells what he knows
• Tells what he has experienced
• Tells what he has actually seen or heard

➤ How did the disciples prepare to witness before the Day of Pentecost? (Acts 2:1)

1. They met together and put away all differences.
2. They believed Christ's promise and prayed in faith.
3. They claimed the endowment of power that Christ had promised.
4. They revealed Christ in their lives.
5. They went forth preaching the Word. (See *The Desire of Ages,* p. 827.)

➤ How did the disciple John witness?

"Christ was alive, when the world began, yet I myself have seen Him with my own eyes and listened to Him speak. I have touched Him with my own hands. He is God's message of Life. This one who is Life from God has been shown to us and we guarantee that we have seen Him; I am speaking of Christ, who is eternal Life.

"He was with the Father and then was shown to us. Again I say, we are telling you about what we ourselves have actually seen and heard, so that you may share the fellowship and the joys we have with the Father and with Jesus Christ His Son."—1 John 1:1-3.

John could witness for Christ because he had . . .

• Seen Christ

• Known Christ

• Heard Christ

When John witnessed, it was a first-hand witness. A witness can only tell what he has seen and experienced.

➤ How did the woman at the well witness?

"Then the woman left her water pot beside the well and went back to the village and told everyone, 'Come and meet a man who told me everything I ever did. Can this be the Messiah?'" —John 4:28-30.

1. Her direct testimony of her experience with Christ was so forceful that the entire city emptied out.

2. Many believed on Christ because of what the woman told them about her encounter with Jesus. (See John 4:39.)

3. When people have a personal encounter with Jesus Christ, they can't help talking about it.

➤ The witness of the man who had been "possessed with the devil"

"As Jesus was getting into the boat, the man who had been demon possessed begged to go with Him. Jesus did not let him, but said, 'Go home to your family and tell them how much the Lord has done for you.' So the man went away and began to tell in the Decapolis how much Jesus had done for him. And all the people were amazed."—Mark 5:19, 20.

1. Jesus told him, "Go home to your family."

2. Jesus told him, "Tell them how much the Lord has done for you."

3. Did he do it? "And he departed, and began to tell in the Decapolis how much Jesus had done for him."

4. What was the impact of this witnessing? "And all the people were amazed." (See *The Desire of Ages,* p. 340.)

5. Christian witnessing is the fruit of a personal confrontation, experience, and relationship with Jesus Christ. When you have this, you can't stop talking about it.

➤ Paul received the same instruction

"You will be his witness to everyone of what you have seen and heard."—Acts 22:15.

Read Acts 26:19 for an example of how Paul witnessed for Jesus. Witnessing became a way of life for Paul.

➤ What "great things has the Lord done" for us that we can witness about?

1. Jesus took our sins away when He died on the cross! —1 John 1:9.

2. He made us acceptable to the King of the universe, who accepts and loves us!—Eph. 1:6.

3. He has given us the Holy Spirit—the gift Jesus promised to send us when He went back to Heaven.—Eph. 1:13.

4. We are born again with a new, divine nature.—John 3:5-8.

5. We have become a part of the family of God and will one day sit with our Lord on His throne, helping in the administration of the universe.—Rev. 3:21.

6. We've been given eternal life. (See 1 John 5:13.) There is no greater gift that man could receive. All other gifts

would be meaningless without eternal life. Read *The Desire of Ages,* pp. 331-338.

7. When we get our minds around the incredible reality of what "great things" Christ has done for us, we won't be concerned about "having to witness." We simply won't be able to keep from witnessing. Read Jeremiah 20:9.

➤ It's important to know that we ourselves are converted

Perhaps you have never made a total and complete commitment of your life to Christ, accepting Him as the Lord and Savior of your life. If so, here is what you need to do.

1. Read *Steps to Christ,* chapter 5, entitled "Faith and Acceptance."

2. Study Lesson 5 of "In His Word"—the Gospel Presentation.

3. Ask your pastor or a friend to pray with you until you have the assurance of acceptance and forgiveness.

➤ You are ready to witness

"Those who have put on Christ will relate their experiences, tracing step by step the leadings of the Holy Spirit—their hungering and thirsting for the knowledge of God and of Jesus Christ whom He has sent, the result of their searching of the Scriptures, their prayers, their soul agony, and the words of Christ to them, 'Your sins are forgiven.' It is unnatural for any to keep these things secret, and those who are filled with the love of Christ will not do so."—*Christ's Object Lessons,* p. 125.

What is the most effective witnessing we can do?

"That which will be most effective is the testimony of our own experience."
—The Desire of Ages, pp. 347, 348.

➤ Your personal testimony: Why should I give a personal testimony?

"Our confession of His faithfulness is Heaven's chosen agency for revealing Christ to those around us. Each one of us has a unique experience from everyone else, and God wants us to share that experience. Our own story, when supported by a Christ-like life, has an irresistible power on those who hear us tell it.

"Thousands can be reached in the most simple and humble way. The most intellectual, those who are looked upon as the world's most gifted men and women, are often refreshed by the simple words of one who loves God, and who can speak of that love as naturally as a worldly person speaks of the things that interest him or her most deeply."—*Christ's Object Lessons,* p. 232.

What will happen if we talk about Christ in our own experience? People will be powerfully drawn to the Savior!

➤ How to prepare your personal testimony

Follow this outline . . .

1. Talk about what your life was like before you met Jesus. (Lonely, insecure, guilt-ridden, aimless, etc.)

2. Share how you found Christ and what the circumstances were. (Evangelistic meetings, Bible studies, friend, tragedy, etc.)

3. Tell how your life has changed since you met Jesus. Describe changes, joys, and blessings. For instance, I found peace, hope for the future, security in knowing God controls my life and the world, etc.

➤ Positive things to emphasize

1. Be prepared to tell others humbly but courageously, "I am a Christian."

2. Keep your testimony brief (three to four minutes).

3. Be enthusiastic and cheerful.

4. If you accepted Christ in your youth, emphasize what your Christian heritage has done for your life, what it has meant to you, how it has solved your problems, given you security, etc.

5. Start with an interest-arousing statement and climax with telling about Christ—what He means to you and what He has done for you.

6. Rehearse your personal witness for Christ so that it "flows" naturally whenever and wherever you may share it.

7. Learn to give your personal testimony in a clear, concise, and coherent manner.

➤ Things to avoid

1. Avoid denominational jargon, which fails to communicate properly. For example: "Since I came into the message," "after I accepted the truth," etc. Use such phrases as, "Since I accepted Christ," "since I became a Christian," or "after I found Christ."

2. Don't glamorize sin by telling in detail how wicked you used to be or the specific things you used to do (smoking, drinking, drugs, immoral living, stealing, etc.) Be general. Say, "Before I found Christ, I did many things that were contrary to God's will." People will feel condemned if you are too specific.

3. Don't be critical of other people or churches.

4. Don't moralize at the end of your testimony by saying, "I know the Lord will do the same for you, if . . ."

5. Don't dwell on the things that you "gave up" to become a Christian. Dwell on the wonderful things Christ has done for you instead.

➤ Phrases you might use

1. "I needed help, and I found it in Jesus. He forgave my sins and took all my guilt away."

2. "I found the Bible to be the voice of God to my soul. It gave me hope for the future—something to look forward to."

3. "In Christ, the hunger of my soul has been satisfied. I am no longer feel lonely or empty."

4. "I still have problems, but I now have Someone who can help me with my problems and give me the strength and courage I need."

5. "Now, every day is a new adventure with Christ. He puts a song in my heart and a smile on my face."

6. "The best decision I have ever made in my life was the decision to accept Christ and follow Him."

"Arouse every spiritual energy to action. Tell those that you visit that the end of all things is at hand. The Lord Jesus Christ will open the door of their hearts, and will make upon their minds lasting impressions."—*Testimonies,* vol. 9, p. 38.

Write out your testimony and practice giving it to a friend

Use the witness worksheet on the next page. Copy the page if you wish and fill it in—then practice giving your personal testimony to a friend.

➤ Personal witness worksheet (fill in): "How I Discovered Life At Its Best"

MY LIFE BEFORE I ACCEPTED CHRIST:
What it was like. How I needed help.

HOW I FOUND CHRIST AND BECAME A CHRISTIAN:
Tell how it happened. "I found the Bible the voice of God to my soul."—*Testimonies,* vol. 8, p. 321.

MY LIFE SINCE I FOUND CHRIST:
Tell of the change, the joys, the blessings. "In Christ, the hunger of my soul has been satisfied."

Winning Their Confidence

It can safely be said that the majority of people living in this country are fearful or suspicious, or both. When you, as a stranger, arrive at their door, they are going to be apprehensive about you and the reason for your being there. If you announce at the very outset the purpose of your mission in so many words, they may reject it without every really understanding the great blessings that you have to offer them. In order to get a fair hearing, so that the prejudices and fears that they have about us and our mission may be disarmed, we need to be very wise in our approach.

One religious leader has said that we must earn the right to ask them personal questions and talk to them about the deepest thoughts they have in their religious life. Let us find the avenue to the heart so that we can gain access to their mind, and then they will be willing to listen to the special message we have to share with them.

One proven, effective way of getting to know people in a way that builds confidence and puts them at ease can be remembered by the acronym F-O-R-T, as follows:

F — Family

The first things you can most easily talk to people about are their families—or themselves. Someone has said that the sweetest word in human language is the name of the person to whom you are talking. Talk to the person about himself and his family, and he will know that you are interested in the same things that he is interested in. This is an excellent time to learn about the various influences that have worked to mold the person with whom you are talking.

Get her to tell you where she was born, where she has lived, how many children she has and where they are, and what they are doing. This will relax her and divert her mind from her fear of you and your mission. You will better understand her and really become acquainted with her as you hear about her life. She will feel that you are really interested in her.

O — Occupation

Most women will be intensely interested in their husbands and children, and most men will usually be interested in their jobs or hobbies. Get the man to tell you about his occupation or what he does for recreation, and he will warm up and open up to you, telling you about the things that really interest him. As he shares with you his interests, you will become his friend. You will discover now that he will share other things with you that he would not have thought of telling you a few minutes before. If the lady of the house works outside the home, she may also like to talk about her work. You will learn a great deal about these people by just listening to what they tell you and also by what they do not say.

R — Religion

We need to know the person's religious background so that we can help him in his religious growth. You might say, "Tell me something about your religious background." This approach lets the person start wherever he is most comfortable and it will give you the opportunity to ask other short questions that will give you a religious profile of the person. This is very valuable information as you will find out if he is a church member, attends church, studies his Bible, etc. This will help you adapt your approach to fit his spiritual needs.

T — Testimony

You have the opportunity to build a bridge by which you can now lead the person to begin thinking about the message of salvation that you have come to share with him. You will not want to preach or exhort, but you can witness to your own relationship with Jesus Christ. (You will have the opportunity to write out your testimony of how you found Christ as your Saviour, and you will be able to share other facets of your life with Christ as you allow the Holy Spirit to lead and direct in your witnessing program.) Try to fit your testimony to some felt need that the person with whom you have been visiting has expressed. Show him or her, by sharing your own experience in Christ, how He has been the answer to a similar problem that you have had in your life. This will help the person want to know the same Saviour who has helped you, and it will help create a feeling of kinship with you as he or she identifies with your problem and the solution you found in Jesus.

➤ Follow Christ's example

"Christ's method alone will give true
success in reaching the people."
—The Ministry of Healing, p. 143.

1. He met the people where they were.

   "Jesus saw in every soul one to whom must be given the
   call to His kingdom. He reached the hearts of the people
   by going among them as one who desired their good. He
   sought them in the public streets, in private houses, on the
   boats, in the synagogue, by the shores of the lake, and at
   the marriage feast. He met them at their daily vocations
   and manifested an interest in their secular affairs. He
   carried His instruction into the household, bringing
   families in their own homes under the influence of His
   divine presence. His strong personal sympathy helped to
   win hearts."—*The Desire of Ages,* p. 151.

2. Wherever He was, He spoke to men of things pertaining to the higher life.

"We should do as Christ did. Wherever He was. . . . He spoke to men of the things pertaining to the higher life. When He opened His lips to speak, their attention was riveted upon Him, and every word was to some soul a savor of life unto life. So it should be with us. Wherever we are, we should watch for opportunities of speaking to others of the Saviour. If we follow Christ's example in doing good, hearts will open to us as they did to Him. Not abruptly, but with tact born of divine love, we can tell them of Him who is the 'chiefest among ten thousand,' and the One 'altogether lovely.' This is the very highest work in which we can employ the talent of speech. It was given to us that we might present Christ as the sin-pardoning Saviour."—*Christ's Object Lessons,* pp. 331, 338.

3. The work of Christ was mostly on a one-to-one basis.

"The work of Christ was largely made up of personal interviews. He had a faithful regard for the one-soul audience. From that one soul the intelligence received was carried to thousands."—*Testimonies,* vol. 6, p. 115.

"One of the most effective ways in which light can be communicated is by private personal effort. In the home circle, at your neighbor's fireside, at the bedside of the sick, in a quiet way you may read the Scriptures and speak a word for Jesus and the truth. Thus you may sow precious seed that will spring up and bring forth fruit." —*Testimonies,* vol. 6, pp. 428, 429.

"The Lord desires that His word of grace shall be brought home to every soul. To a great degree this must be accomplished by personal labor. This was Christ's method."—*Christ's Object Lessons,* p. 229.

"By personal labor reach those around you. Become acquainted with them. Preaching will not do the work that needs to be done. Angels of God attend you to the dwellings of those you visit. This work cannot be done by proxy. Money lent or given will not accomplish it. Sermons will not do it. By visiting the people, talking, praying, sympathizing with them you will win hearts. This is the highest missionary work that you can do. To do it, you will need resolute, persevering faith, unwearying patience, and a deep love for souls."—*Testimonies,* vol. 9, p. 41.

4. He spoke words of sympathy and kindness and encouragement, sharing their burdens.

"He spoke a word of sympathy here and a word there, as He saw men weary, yet compelled to bear heavy burdens. He shared their burdens, and repeated to them the lessons He had learned from nature, of the love, the kindness, the goodness of God. . . . He sought to inspire with hope the most rough and unpromising, setting before them the assurance that they might become blameless and harmless, attaining such a character as would make them manifest as the children of God. Often He met those who had drifted under Satan's control, and who had no power to break from his snare. To such a one, discouraged, sick, tempted, and fallen, Jesus would speak words of tenderest pity, words that were needed and could be understood. Others He met who were fighting a hand-to-hand battle with the adversary of souls. These He encouraged to persevere, assuring them that they would win; for angels of God were on their side, and would give them the victory."
—*The Desire of Ages,* p. 91.

5. He passed by no human being as worthless or hopeless.

"He passed by no human being as worthless, but applied the saving remedy to every soul. In whatever company He found Himself, He presented a lesson appropriate to the time and the circumstances.

"He walked among the thoughtless, the rude, and the uncourteous; amid the unjust publicans, the reckless prodigals, the unrighteous Samaritans, the heathen soldiers, the rough peasants, and the mixed multitude."
—*The Desire of Ages*, p. 91.

6. He taught that all had talents to be used to God's glory.

    "He taught all to look upon themselves as endowed with precious talents, which if rightly employed would secure for them eternal riches. He weeded all vanity from life, and by His own example taught that every moment of time is fraught with eternal results; that it is to be cherished as a treasure, and to be employed for holy purposes."
    —*The Desire of Ages*, p. 91.

7. He ministered to the poor and rich alike.

    "While He ministered to the poor, Jesus studied also to find ways of reaching the rich. He sought the acquaintance of the wealthy and cultured Pharisee, the Jewish nobleman, and Roman ruler. He accepted their invitations, attended their feasts, made Himself familiar with their interests and occupations, that He might gain access to their hearts, and reveal to them the imperishable riches."—*The Ministry of Healing*, pp. 24, 25.

8. Christ's power in gentleness and humility won hearts.

    "Our Saviour's power was not in a strong array of sharp words that would pierce through the very soul; it was His gentleness and His plain, unassuming manner that made Him a conqueror of hearts."—*Testimonies*, vol. 3, p. 477.

9.   Christ was social.

"The example of Christ in linking Himself with the interests of humanity should be followed by all who preach His word, and by all who have received the gospel of His grace. We are not to renounce social communion. We should not seclude ourselves from others. In order to reach all classes, we must meet them where they are. They will seldom seek us of their own accord. Not alone from the pulpit are the hearts of men touched by divine truths. There is another field of labor, humbler, it may be, but fully as promising. It is found in the home of the lowly, and in the mansion of the great; at the hospitable board and in gatherings for innocent social enjoyment."—*The Desire of Ages,* p. 152.

"Social power, sanctified by the grace of Christ, must be employed in winning souls to the Saviour."—*The Desire of Ages,* p. 152.

➤ Whom should we approach?

"Go to your neighbors one by one, and come close to them till their hearts are warmed by your unselfish interest and love. Sympathize with them, pray with them, watch for opportunities to do them good, and as you can, gather a few together and open the Word of God to the darkened minds. Keep watching, as he who must render an account for the souls of men, and make the most the privileges that God gives you of laboring with Him in His moral vineyard."—*Review and Herald,* March 13, 1888.

"My brethren and sisters, visit those who live near you, and by sympathy and kindness seek to reach their hearts. Be sure to work in a way that will remove prejudice instead of creating it. And remember that those who know the truth for this time, and yet confine their efforts to their own churches, refusing to work for their unconverted neighbors, will be called to account for unful-filled duties."—*Testimonies,* vol. 9, p. 134.

➤ Conclusion

The results of following these methods of Christ can be seen in the following statement:

> *"If we would humble ourselves before God,*
> *and be kind and courteous and tender-*
> *hearted and pitiful, there would be one*
> *hundred conversions to the truth*
> *where now there is only one."*
> —Testimonies, vol. 9, p. 189.

Christ—the Center and Theme of All We Do

"And I, if I be lifted up, will draw
all men unto me."
—John 12:32

"Of all professing Christians, Seventh-day Adventists should be foremost in uplifting Christ before the world."—*Gospel Workers,* p. 156.

"The very first and most important thing is to melt and subdue the soul by presenting our Lord Jesus Christ as the sin-pardoning Savior."—*Testimonies,* vol. 6, p. 54.

"The love of Jesus will melt and win hearts when the mere reiteration of doctrine will accomplish nothing."—*The Desire of Ages,* p. 826.

"Present Jesus because you know Him as your personal Savior. Let His melting love, His rich grace flow forth from human lips. You need not present doctrinal points unless questioned. But take the Word, and with tender, yearning love for souls, show them the precious righteousness of Christ, to whom you and they must come to be saved."—*Evangelism,* p. 442.

"Bear with a certain voice an affirmative message. Lift Him up, the Man of Calvary, higher and still higher. There is power in the exaltation of the cross of Christ."—Letter 65, 1905.

"There is one great central truth to be kept ever before the mind in searching the Scriptures—Christ and Him crucified. Every other truth is invested with influence and power corresponding to its relation to this theme. It is only in the light of the cross that we can discern the exalted character of the law of God. The soul palsied by sin can be endowed with life only through the work wrought out upon the cross by the Author of our salvation. The love of Christ constrains man to unite with Him in His labors and sacrifice. The revelation of divine love awakens in them a sense of their neglected obligation to be light bearers to the world, and inspires them with a missionary spirit. This truth enlightens the mind and sanctifies the soul. It will banish unbelief and inspire faith. . . . When Christ in His work of redemption is seen to be the great central truth of the system of truth, a new light is shed upon all the events of the past and future. They are seen in a new relation, and possess a new and deeper significance."—*That I May Know Him,* p. 208.

The last words of Christ to His disciples are found in Acts:

"But ye shall receive power, after that the Holy Ghost is come upon you: and ye shall be witnesses unto Me both in Jerusalem, and in all Judea, and in Samaria, and unto the uttermost part of the earth."—Acts 1:8.

Christ told the disciples that they would receive power to witness about Him.

1. He told them that He had all power. Matt. 28:19.

2. He told them that they would receive power as the Holy Ghost came upon them. Acts 1:8.

3. He told them why this power would be given them—to assist them in witnessing about Him. Acts 1:8.

4. When the Holy Ghost came upon them, they "began to speak." Acts 2:4.

Many people emphasize the "tongues" part of this text, but the important thing was not the language but the message.

➤ Message of the early church

What was the message the early church shared with the people in their witnessing?

Christ was the center and theme of their witnessing. They did not talk about the weather, the temple, or the city of Jerusalem. They talked about the One they loved—the One who filled their every thought and plan.

1. Read the following texts: Acts 2:21-24, 36; Acts 3:1-6, 26; Acts 4:9-33; Acts 5:27-42; Acts 7:59, 60.

2. They constantly uplifted Christ!

➤ Lift Him up

Years ago, we were instructed to be foremost in lifting up the Savior.

1. "Of all professing Christians, Seventh-day Adventists should be foremost in uplifting Christ before the world."
   —*Gospel Workers,* p. 156 (1915 edition).

2. "Lift up Jesus, you that, teach the people, lift Him up in sermon, in song, in prayer: Let all your powers be directed to pointing souls confused, bewildered, lost, to 'the Lamb of God.'"

   "Lift Him up, the risen Savior. Hold forth the word of life, presenting Jesus as the hope of the penitent and the stronghold of every believer. Reveal the way of peace to the troubled and the despondent, and show forth the grace and completeness of the Savior."—*Gospel Workers,* p. 159 (1915 edition).

➤ Share the good news

We have assumed that people know that Christ is the Savior, so we have spent most of our time presenting doctrines of the church, which in many cases may have convinced but not converted. How little we are doing in sharing the good news that He is the One who saves and satisfies!

1. "Often doctrinal subjects are presented with no special effect; for men expect others to press upon them their doctrines; but when the matchless love of Christ is dwelt upon, His grace impresses the heart. There are many who are sincerely seeking for light, who know not what they must do to be saved. Oh, tell them the love of God, of the sacrifice made on Calvary's cross to save the perishing." —*Colporteur Ministry,* p. 42.

2. "Great wisdom is required in dealing with human minds, even in giving a reason of the hope that is within us. What is the hope of which we are to give a reason? The hope of eternal life through Jesus Christ. You dwell too much upon special ideas and doctrines, and the heart of the unbeliever is not softened. To try to impress him is like striking upon cold iron."—*Evangelism,* p. 247.

➤ Christ first

We are not to present controversial truths before presenting Christ; we are to present Christ first and then teach the truth as it is in Jesus.

1. "Do not make prominent those features of the message which are a condemnation of the customs and practices of the people, until they have opportunity to know that we are believers in Christ, that we believe in His divinity and in His pre-existence. Let the testimony of the world's Redeemer be dwelt upon."—*Testimonies,* vol. 6, p. 58 (1900 edition).

2. "If Christ is presented as the Savior of the world, the seed sown may spring up and bear fruit to the glory of God. But often the cross of Calvary is not presented before the people. Some may be listening to the last sermon they will ever hear, and the golden opportunity lost, is lost forever. If in connection with the theory of the truth, Christ and His redeeming love had been proclaimed, these might have been won to His side."—Gospel Workers, pp. 157, 158 (1915 edition).

Draw the illustration (below and following page) of building the wall showing doctrines first (the wrong way), then Christ first (the correct way) to implement a Christ-centered approach.

NOT THIS. . .

BUT THIS

How the Work Will Be Finished

➤ Who?

"Servants of God, with their faces lighted up and shining with holy consecration, will hasten from place to place to proclaim the message from heaven. By thousands of voices, all over the earth, the warning will be given. Miracles will be wrought, the sick will be healed, and signs and wonders will follow the believers."—*The Great Controversy,* p. 612.

➤ What?

"In visions of the night representations passed before me of a great reformatory movement among God's people. Many were praising God. The sick were healed, and other miracles were wrought. A spirit of intercession was seen, even as was manifested before the great day of Pentecost. Hundreds and thousands were seen visiting families, and opening before them the word of God. Hearts were convicted by the power of the Holy Spirit, and a spirit of genuine conversion was manifest. On every side doors were thrown open to the proclamation of the truth. The world seemed to be lightened with the heavenly influence. Great blessings were received by the true and humble people of God." —*Testimonies,* vol. 9, p. 126.

➤ How?

"A great work can be done by presenting to the people the Bible just as it reads. Carry the Word of God to every man's door, urge its plain statements upon every man's conscience, repeat to all the Saviour's command, 'Search the Scriptures.' Admonish them to take the Bible as it is, to implore the divine enlightenment, and then, when the light shines, to gladly accept each precious ray, and fearlessly abide the consequences."—*Review and Herald,* July 10, 1883.

➤ Where?

"There are many who are reading the Scriptures who cannot understand their true import. All over the world men and women are looking wistfully to heaven. Prayers and tears and inquiries go up from souls longing for light, for grace, for the Holy Spirit. Many are on the verge of the kingdom, waiting only to be gathered in."—*Testimonies to Ministers,* p. 109.

A Simple Method of Giving Bible Studies

➤ How to get started

1. If possible, attend a witnessing seminar or training class where you can secure instruction in the art of sharing Christ with others. Study the instructions in this manual carefully and prayerfully.

2. You should have your own Gift Bible and set of "In His Word" lessons.

    a. Place the lessons in a notebook (notebook may be obtained through Seminars Unlimited—817-641-3643).

    b. Study each lesson carefully, filling in the answers in each blank. This will help you to become familiar with the material you will be studying with your student.

    c. Watch for interesting illustrations that you can write into your lessons to share with the student. This will make your studies more meaningful to your student.

    d. In the introduction to each lesson, underline any special thought you might wish to emphasize with your student.

3. Pray earnestly for heavenly wisdom and guidance as you go to study with your student.

    a. "In working for perishing souls, you have the companionship of angels. Thousands upon thousands and ten thousand times ten thousand angels are waiting to co-operate with members of our churches in communicating the light that God has generously given, that a people may be prepared for the coming of Christ."—*Testimonies,* vol. 9, p. 129.

b. "In this work all the angels of heaven are ready to cooperate. All the resources of heaven are at the command of those who are seeking to save the lost. Angels will help you to reach the most careless and the most hardened."—*Christ's Object Lessons,* p. 197.

4. Ask your pastor or personal ministries leader to introduce you to a student with whom you can study.

➤ Gift Bible program

When making contact with someone interested in studying the Bible, it is very helpful to provide a Bible that is paged to correspond to the lessons they are studying.

1. Explain to the student that while they are more than welcome to use their own Bible, you are loaning them a Gift Bible to use because of the special pagination system, which makes it so easy for them to locate the Bible texts quickly. This is very important, because most people have a hard time finding the texts in the Bible. If they have to spend too much time and it seems difficult to them, they will lose interest and feel it is too hard to study the Bible.

2. Tell them that when they have completed the set of lessons, the Bible will become theirs to keep.

3. Tell the student to look up the texts and then to fill in each blank with his answers, and that you will come back the next week and bring the next two lessons and see how he

is doing. (Try to get everyone in the home to study, if possible.)

4. Be certain to make an appointment with the student for the following week. You might ask, "What would be a convenient time for me to come by next week? Is this a good day and time?" Write down the time he says will be convenient and ask for his telephone number—and give him your number. This will save a lot of time.

➤ At the student's home

INTRODUCTION: (If this is your first visit and someone else has left the first two lessons).

1. Introduce yourself, explaining that you have come to deliver the next two lessons and check on progress in studying the Bible in this manner. (Smile and act as if you expect to be let in.)

2. If the student does not let you in, you might say, "Perhaps it would be easier if I just step in a few minutes and go over your lessons with you."

➤ Breaking the ice

1. You might ask, "How did you get along with the lessons this week?" Or, "Did you learn anything new from the lessons?" Or, "Did you enjoy doing the lessons?"

2. Regardless of the answer, take out your notebook and Bible and tell the student that you've studied the lessons yourself and you'd like to quickly go over the lessons together. You could ask, "Perhaps it would be easier and

quicker if I just read the questions and you read the answers from your lessons, OK?"

3. When the student has his lessons and you are ready to start the study, say, "I'd love to have a short prayer before we begin our study." Then quickly bow your head and say a short prayer. You might say, "Our Father, we pray that you will send your Holy Spirit to be with us today as we study Your Word. Help us that we might understand Your plan for this world and for our lives. In Jesus' name. Amen."

Now, you are ready to begin your study. If you have underlined something of special interest in the Introduction, bring this point to your student's attention. If not, comment on the lesson in general. You might say on the first lesson, "With all the problems going on in the world around us, most people wonder if there is anything we can trust." Then read the first question, letting the student read his answer. Go through the complete lesson, reading every question and letting the student read his answers. This is extremely important! You cannot know for sure what he is thinking if you do not do this. Also, this gives you the opportunity to become acquainted with him.

➤ Using audio-visual aids with your Bible studies

In our media-rich age, using audio-visual material can really enhance a student's grasp of biblical truth. When the student can see a presentation of the particular subject as well as studying it from the Bible, it will make twice the impact.

There are numerous sets of materials that can be used to reinforce the Bible studies in various formats, including video, Powerpoint, and even DVD. Often these materials are topical, and with a correlation sheet, can be adapted to work with a number of sets of lesson guides. (Contact Seminars Unlimited for current information.)

One of the most popular media sets currently is the DVD series *New Beginnings,* which has been correlated to a variety of lessons including Revelation and Prophecy lessons in addition to a new set entitled *In His Word.* Recently, the DVD program has been formulated into a 13-tape video program also called *In His Word.* The videos have two programs on each video cassette and are arranged to match the *In His Word* Bible study set of lessons.

The following is one way of using media and lessons together: When you deliver the first two lessons of the course to the student, you should also give him a video tape which will have the same two subjects on the video that are to be studied. Invite the student, after he has done his first lesson, to view the first video. When he has finished the second lesson, he should view the second video. This will present vital supplemental material that really reinforces what has been studied.

Inform the student that you will return at the agreed time and that if he has any questions, you will take a few minutes and answer them. When you come back at the appointed time, tell the student that you have been studying these lessons too and it would help to just go over your answers together. You read the questions, and let the student give his answers. You may wish to ask if he had any questions on the video program he has watched.

When you have finished going over both lessons, compliment him on the great job he has done in studying his lessons and leave him the next two lessons and the next video. Then make the appropriate appeal when you have completed the lesson.

You will find that this method of study is most productive and will bring you faster results.

Salvation in the Present Tense

"Today if ye will hear His voice,
harden not your heart."
—Heb. 3:15.

"Behold now is the accepted time; behold,
now is the day of salvation."
—2 Cor. 6:2.

"Many will be lost while hoping and desir-
ing to be Christians. They do not come to the
point of yielding the will to God. They do not
now choose to be Christians."
—Steps to Christ, p. 48.

➤ The gospel presentation

Near the close of the study on the gospel, ask the question, "Is there any good reason that you would not like to receive Jesus as your Saviour *now* so you can have the assurance of eternal life?"

1. If the person says, "Yes, there is," then ask, "Would you mind sharing with me what some of these obstacles might be?" If the person says that he would rather not, then give the assurance that you will continue to pray for him that he might be able to make a decision soon.

2. If the person says, "No, there is no good reason," then continue by telling the student that he can commit his life to the Lord right now by telling God about his decision.

42

3. Suggest that you kneel together (if possible) and tell God of his decision.

4. You lead in prayer, thanking God for the gift of salvation and the sacrifice of Christ. Thank God for making it possible for all of us to have eternal life. Then pause and ask the student if he would not like to tell God in his own words of the decision that he has made.

5. If the student hesitates, suggest that he tell God in his own words what this decision means:

   a. Please forgive me for all my sins.

   b. I want to receive Jesus as my Savior and Lord right now.

   c. I want to invite You to come into my life and live in my heart.

   d. Thank You for saving me and making me Your child.

6. If he does not know how to pray, suggest that you will lead in prayer and that he can repeat after you. Here is a suggested prayer:

   "Dear God, please forgive all of my sins. [Pause] I want to invite You to take control of my life. [Pause] I want Jesus to come into my heart. [Pause] I want Him to be the Saviour and the Lord of my life. [Pause] Thank You for giving me eternal life in Jesus. [Pause] In Jesus' name I pray. Amen."

7. Your prayer following his should be very short and simple —thanking God for the student's decision.

8. Then you could say, "Welcome to the family of God! You've just made the greatest decision of your life!" If the student has not read *Steps to Christ,* this would be a good time to leave this book with him.

Helpful Suggestions for Various Situations During the Bible Study

➤ Don't pose as an authority on the Bible

1. Be a "learner" along with the student so he will feel relaxed with you. Tell him you are studying the Bible too.

2. This will also take a load off your shoulders, because he won't expect you to know everything.

➤ Try not to let the study become too complicated or involved

1. "Jesus did not use long and difficult words in His discourses. He used plain language, adapted to the minds of the common people. He went no farther into the subject He was expounding than they were able to follow Him." —*Gospel Workers,* p. 169.

   "The greatest Teacher the world has ever known was the most definite, simple, and practical in His instruction." —*Gospel Workers,* p. 50.

2. If you make the study too lengthy, the student may feel he just doesn't have the time to study with you. You should be able to study the two lessons and be on your way in one hour.

➤ If the student has a wrong answer

Don't say, "That's wrong." Say in a very kind way, "We seem to have different thoughts on that question. Let's read that text again to be sure what the Bible says." Have the student read the text in his own Bible, then read the question. Usually the student will see the right answer immediately.

➤ If the student asks a question you can't answer

Don't be embarrassed. Just say, "I've never thought of that in just that way. I'll try to find the Bible answer and bring it to you next week." Or, you might say, "I'm not certain where that text is, (or what the answer to that question is) but if there is an answer, I'll try to find it in my concordance or Bible dictionary and bring it to you when I come next week."

1. When you have a question on a particular subject and you have to look up the answer or text, write this down on that particular lesson sheet so you will have the answer the next time a student asks you. Before long you will have written down in your lesson sheets most of the questions people ask.

2. There are some questions that cannot be answered because the Bible does not give the answer. You will just have to frankly admit that as far as you know, the Bible does not give the answer. You can say, "We'll have to make a list of these questions and ask the Lord for the answer when we see Him."

3. Never try to answer a question if you don't know the answer. You will find yourself in an embarrassing position, and the student will lose confidence in you.

4. When answering questions, make certain you have the Bible text to back it up. Don't make statements that can be backed up only by the Spirit of Prophecy, as the student will not recognize that authority.

➤ Study the lessons in the order given

Follow the order of lessons as given. These lessons have been carefully compiled in such a way as to lay a foundation for the controversial subjects before they are presented. Experience has revealed that if certain controversial topics are presented before a foundation has been built, many students will drop out of the Bible study program.

Leave at least two lessons each week unless the person is a slow reader or cannot do two each week. You need to keep up a certain momentum, and two lessons work much better than one.

➤ Don't let the student sidetrack you

Keep the student on the subject you are studying at the time. If he asks you about the Sabbath, pork, etc., just say, "That subject will be coming up before very long, and I don't want to spoil your study before we get to it." This will help to avoid controversial topics before the student has sufficient background to understand or accept them.

Another reason for keeping to the study you are having and avoiding other questions is that it weakens the study you are having—and they may miss the whole point of the lesson. It is like taking all the exits on a freeway: You might never arrive at your destination!

➤ Give your student an honest compliment

Always give your student an honest compliment at the end of your study. You might comment, "Say, you really did a great job on these lessons!" Or you might say, "I know you enjoyed the lessons, because you did such a beautiful job with them. As you study more of the lessons, you will enjoy them even more. They just seem to get better as you get farther into them."

This will help build interest and keep them studying. Any lesson they question about that comes later, build up the lesson by saying, "We'll be studying that lesson before long. It's a really exciting lesson, and I know you will really enjoy it."

➤ Never preach, sermonize, moralize, or condemn

1. Don't give the impression that you are "holier than thou." Let the student know that you are also human—that you make mistakes too, that you aren't perfect, but that you are striving for perfection with the Lord's help. Be humble, tenderhearted, and sympathetic. Many of these people are loaded down with heavy burdens and broken hearts. Be gentle.

   "Our Savior's power was not in a strong array of sharp words that would pierce through the very soul; it was His gentleness and His plain, unassuming manner that made Him a conqueror of hearts."—*Testimonies,* vol. 3, p. 477.

2. Never condemn or act shocked at the behavior or sinful practices or language of the student or his children. Never show disapproval of his manners or the condition of his home.

a. "It was a continual pain to Christ to be brought into contact with enmity, depravity, and impurity; but never did He utter one expression to show that His sensibilities were shocked or His refined tastes offended. Whatever the evil habits, the strong prejudices, or the overbearing passions of human beings, He met them all with pitying tenderness. As we partake of His Spirit, we shall regard all men as brethren, with similar temptations and trials, often falling, and struggling to rise again, battling with discouragements and difficulties, craving sympathy and help. Then we shall meet them in such a way as not to discourage or repel them, but to awaken hope in their heart."—*The Ministry of Healing,* pp. 165, 166.

b. "It is always humiliating to have one's errors pointed out. None should make the experience more bitter by needless censure. No one was ever reclaimed by reproach; but many have thus been repelled, and have been led to steel their hearts against conviction. A tender spirit, a gentle, winning deportment, may save the erring, and hide a multitude of sins."—*The Ministry of Healing,* pp. 165, 166.

➤ Take a friend with you

There are five good reasons for taking a friend with you when it is possible:

1. If there are small children in the home that will interfere with the study, the friend can entertain the children while you have an uninterrupted study.

2. You will be teaching this friend how to give studies, and if you have to be away or ill, you can get your friend to give

the study for you. The friend will already know the student and can easily fill in for you.

3. It is most important not to miss a study. If you fail to go a week or two, it may lessen the interest of your student. Make certain someone takes over your study if you cannot take it.

4. By taking a friend with you (or different friends with you at different times) the student will already know a number of different people in the church when they come to visit.

5. Prayer is the most powerful force in the universe! Having a friend with you who is silently praying while you are conducting the study is of immeasurable worth.

➤ Make sure Christ is at the center of every Bible study

When you are sharing with people, make your emphasis Jesus and Him crucified. Let them know they are a blood-bought soul of the King of the universe. You will find power when you present the cross of Jesus Christ to people. Their hearts will be touched.

➤ Invite your student

Invite your student to visit church—and have Sabbath with them. Do so after your study on the Sabbath. Invite them home for lunch. This is the easiest way to get them to attend church. Usually the student is honored to have you invite him to church and then to lunch.

This is a good way to help the student see how you celebrate the Sabbath. Make it a joyous experience.

➤ Keep your pastor posted

1. Be certain that you keep your pastor posted on the progress of your student.

2. Make certain you introduce your pastor to the student when you bring him to church.

3. Invite the student to attend the Pastor's Bible Class. This is very important. This is the best way to get the student into the church program.

➤ What if the student doesn't have the lessons completed?

1. There are several reasons why the student may not do the lessons:

   a. He may have forgotten about them or has been too busy.

   b. He may not have been sufficiently motivated.

   c. He may have not really understood how to do the lessons.

2. Whatever the reason, you will need to do some encouraging.

   a. You might say, "Oh, that's too bad! I know you will really enjoy these lessons when you get into them—they are very interesting. Well, I'll tell you what we can do. Since I have already set aside this time just for you, why don't I step in, and we will do one of the lessons together? You'll see how quick and easy it is, and then next time we can get both of the lessons done."

b. Go in, and go through one lesson with the student, showing how easy it is and how quickly you can study this way. Then leave one more lesson with the student so he will have two to do that week. Often people will take off and have no more problems.

Do not be discouraged if you find some students who quite routinely do not have their lessons completed when you arrive.

The reasons, as noted earlier, can be many. Some people habitually procrastinate. Others are forgetful. Still others are easily distracted by other things during the week.

You may find that some respond to just a few words of positive encouragement as they are getting started with the lessons and then move forward to complete their remaining lessons on time each week. You may also find those who will need your ongoing motivation nearly every week.

And do not be discouraged, either, if some who begin the lessons choose not to continue. Not all will respond to the spiritual invitations that come their way. But as the Holy Spirit continues to work in their lives, they may be more open to such invitations at a later time. As one well-known Adventist evangelist of a decade gone by used to say, "No use tugging in vain on green fruit. Give it more time. God has plenty of other fruit that's already ripe."

How to Succeed in Giving Bible Studies

"Without me you can do nothing."
—John 15:5.

➤ The power and presence of the Holy Spirit

In order to succeed in this work, we must have the power and presence of the Holy Spirit. We can only have this as we spend time in studying the Scriptures and communing with God.

1. "Without a living faith in Christ as a personal Savior, it is impossible to make your faith felt in a skeptical world. If you would draw sinners out of the swift-running current, your own feet must not stand on slippery places."—*Gospel Workers,* p. 274.

2. "It is a sin for those who attempt to teach the Word to others to be themselves neglectful of its study."—*Gospel Workers,* p. 249.

➤ Never think of failure

Be optimistic. Never think or talk of failure. God is responsible for the results when we do our best.

"When we give ourselves wholly to God, and in our work follow His directions, He makes Himself responsible for its accomplishment. He would not have us conjecture as to the success of our honest endeavors. Not once should we even think of failure. We are to cooperate with One who knows no failure."—*Christ's Object Lessons,* p. 363.

➤ The rewards of service

1. Rejoicing NOW.

    As the student progresses in his study, he will show more
    enthusiasm each week that you study with him. What a
    thrill it will be to see the opening of the student's mind and
    heart to the influence of the Holy Spirit! There can be no
    greater joy than to help a person surrender his life and will
    to our Lord Jesus Christ.

2. Rejoicing LATER.

    "The redeemed will meet and recognize those whose
    attention they have directed to the uplifted Savior. What a
    blessed conversation they will have with these souls. "I
    was a sinner," it will be said, "without God and without
    hope in the world; and you came to me, and drew my
    attention to the precious Savior as my only hope. You read
    to me the precious promises of God's Word. You inspired
    in me faith that He would save me. My heart was softened,
    subdued, broken, as I contemplated the sacrifice which
    Christ had made for me."—*Gospel Workers,* p. 518.

    "What rejoicing there will be as these redeemed ones meet
    those who have had a burden in their behalf; how their
    hearts will thrill with satisfaction."—*Gospel Workers,*
    p. 519.

➤ The advantages of this simple Bible study plan

1. You can easily and effectively learn to use this simple
    method of giving Bible studies in a short period of time.

2. You have the opportunity to come close to the students and get acquainted with them and learn their thinking. This gives you the ability to find your way to their hearts.

   "Your success will not depend so much upon your knowledge and accomplishments, as upon your ability to find your way to the heart. By being social and coming close to the people, you may turn the current of their thoughts more readily than by the most able discourse." —*Gospel Workers,* p. 193.

3. The student learns to study the Scriptures on his own, by himself. By using the pagination system, the student can quickly and easily find the answers from the Bible itself, comparing scripture with scripture. As he reads the answers from the Bible, the Holy Spirit works on his mind and heart. His faith is strengthened, and confidence in our message is increased.

   "God designs that men shall not decide from impulse, but from weight of evidence, carefully comparing scripture with scripture."—*The Desire of Ages,* p. 458.

4. This system takes less time to study with people, so you will be able to reach more people. The student has already studied the material, so it is a matter of going over each question and discussing his answers and answering his questions. You do not have to spend the time looking up all the texts.

5. The student actually retains more by using this method of Bible study, because he goes over the material three times:

   a. He reads the answers to the questions from the Bible.

   b. He writes the answers to each question.

c. He repeats the answers to you as you go over the questions together, so he hears himself give the answer.

Thus, we have used avenues of learning recommended by many psychologists, who believe that we retain 10 percent of what we hear; 30 percent of what we see and hear; and 90 percent of what we see, hear, and repeat. The percentage is greatly increased by this method of study.

6. The student can become an instructor himself when he finishes his lessons. He has already done the lessons, and he has his notebook with the corrected lessons already. Many students have used their lessons and given studies to their loved ones and friends with great success.

"He who begins with a little knowledge, in a humble way, and tells what he knows, while seeking diligently for further knowledge, will find the whole heavenly treasure awaiting his demand. The more he seeks to impart light, the more light he will receive. The more one tries to explain the Word of God to others, with a love for souls, the plainer it becomes to himself. The more we use our knowledge and exercise our powers, the more knowledge and power we shall have."—*Christian Service,* p. 100.

Encourage your student to share. Tell your student that everyone who is born into God's kingdom is a missionary. Encourage him to start studying with friends and loved ones as soon as he becomes a part of God's family.

How to Get People Into Bible Studies

> ➤ **Strangers—or casual acquaintances?**

In developing the interest of persons you meet and get acquainted with, it will be necessary for you to get them either to read or study. The Holy Spirit will speak to their hearts as they let their minds dwell on spiritual things.

If the person is not interested in studying the Bible when you first meet him, it would be well to have two or three interesting small booklets, such as *Nick's Discovery,* that you could leave with him to read. These stories will touch his heart and create a desire in him to study more deeply into the things of God.

Before people become Seventh-day Adventists, it will be necessary for you to get them into the study of the Bible so they can really understand God's plan for their lives and for the world. You should be looking for an opening to get them into Bible studies as soon as possible. Perhaps a good time would be when you first talk to them and use the F-O-R-T approach.

You will want to tell them in your testimony about the wonderful change that came into your life as you really became acquainted with God's Word. Your testimony can be tailored so that you can lead them to feel their need of an in-depth understanding of God's plan of salvation. Then you might ask, "Have you ever studied the Bible by subject? It's really fascinating."

Then suggest to them that you have a simple, systematic way by which they can study the Bible by subject. Explain how it works. You might say, "Each lesson is really exciting, and I know you will really enjoy every one of them. They get more interesting as you go along. You really have a treat in store for you as you study these lessons." (Be enthusiastic. Much depends upon your ability to "sell" the idea of studying the lessons and sufficiently motivate them at this time.)

➤ Bible study response cards—"Something Wonderful for You"

By far one of the most productive tools to enlist interests in Bible Studies is a Bible Study Response Card such as the one entitled "Something Wonderful for You." It has been distributed by the millions in various forms, colors, and offers. Seminars Unlimited is one of the suppliers of this economical tool, which can be hand distributed or direct mailed for less than half the cost of a first-class stamp. For details and samples, contact Seminars Unlimited at 814-641-3643.

Seminars Unlimited can also provide the number of residential addresses for any given zip code across the country. Responses usually average about 10 to 25 per thousand mailed, but one church in Texas received over 839 responses for an average mailing.

➤ Contacting those in your neighborhood

Surveys: A simple multi-question survey can prove very effective in securing Bible study interests as individuals go door to door in their own neighborhood. The survey is a vehicle to start a conversation rather than a "census bureau" statistics tool. With a friendly smile and some conversational ability, individuals have gotten as high as half those surveyed to at least start Bible studies.

Door hangers: Another approach, as you are on your daily exercise route, is to pray for the individuals in each of the homes as you pass by. Prayer is not only powerful but often very much desired by those around us. People often have an emotional response when they learn they are being prayed for. By letting them know that they are the object of your concern and prayers, doors often open, and people become more receptive to your invitations to study the Bible with you. An attractive little door hanger is available that can be left for them, on which they can check prayer requests for special needs or the desire to start studying the Bible. This can be left on the door or handed to them in person.

Prospectus method: A prospectus is a simple, easy-to-use method of getting people into the Bible study plan by going from door to door. The one prospecting obtains a sufficient number of prospectus pamphlets to cover every home in one or two blocks. He then puts an enrollment card into the inside pocket of the prospectus and knocks on the door of each home in that block.

He greets the occupant warmly and says he has something special that he would like to leave with them for their consideration. He mentions that he would appreciate it if they would look it over and read it through and that he will return and pick it up in approximately an hour.

When he returns, if the individual has signed the enrollment card indicating his desire to take advantage of the offer for Bible studies, he then leaves the Bible and first two lessons and explains how the program works.

This eliminates the necessity of a "hard sell" and gives the opportunity to every person living in that block to study God's Word if he is interested in doing so. This is a very "low key" and effective way to secure Bible studies.

A variation uses a video instead of the booklet. The approach works the same for either media.

Ads: Often a small ad in the classified section of the local newspaper has proved fruitful. Bargain shoppers and regional papers are usually very economically priced.

Personal contacts: Remember that all the media and advertising cannot take the place of the personal touch. In your daily contact with those around you, be ever mindful of opportunities to ask someone to study with you. People are open to helping each other when asked. One approach is to simply request help in learning about the Bible. "I need someone to study the Bible with me." "I have gotten a set of lesson guides, and I need a study partner." Would you be willing to please help me by being my study partner?" You would be amazed how many people will respond to a simple request such as this.

➤ Working with media names

One small church in Wisconsin got 72 requests asking for Bible studies, utilizing media names. A letter is sent to all It Is Written, Amazing Facts, Voice of Prophecy, and other media names in your area offering free Bible study guides to those who are really interested in studying God's Word by subject. A response card is enclosed. When the response card is returned, the study team goes to place the Bible and lessons with the interest, explaining how the program works. They return each week and study the lessons with the student.

One church phones the various media names, stating that they are representatives of that program. They then ask if the person being phoned has heard about the Bible study guide offer being made by the program to all those who might be interested in studying the Bible by subject. If the person phoned is really interested in finding out God's plan for the world and for their lives, they are told that the one making the call will be happy to drop by with the guides and explain how they work. The guides are free, it is explained, and there is no cost to them now or ever. (You could use the prospectus or simply explain the program when you follow up this name.)

When you visit the home of someone who has had contact with one of the television or radio programs, you should introduce yourself by saying that you represent that particular program and that you just wanted to share the good news about an exciting way to study the Bible by subject. It is good to carry a piece of literature from that program that you can leave with the listener.

Working for Missing and Inactive Members

"I will heal their backsliding,
I will love them freely."
—Hosea 14:4.

➤ Christ loved missing and inactive members

Christ spent a good share of His ministry here on earth trying to reach and reclaim the missing and inactive members of His day. In Luke 15, He gave three parables through which He intended to teach a needed lesson to the religious leaders of His age. The religious leaders taught that God rejoiced when a sinner, or missing member, was destroyed. Christ showed by the three parables that God is waiting for the lost to be found and reclaimed. He said that there is rejoicing in heaven when one lost sinner is found and rescued.

In Luke 15, Christ talks about three different types of missing members:

1. Those who, like the sheep, knew they were lost but didn't know how to find their way back. Someone had to go and search for them and bring them back.

2. Those who, like the coin, didn't realize they were lost, so they were unable to do anything about their condition.

3. Those who, like the prodigal son, know they are lost, know their way back, but are afraid they will not be received back and forgiven. Most inactive Seventh-day Adventists will fit into this category. We need to share with them a positive, reassuring message that our heavenly Father loves

them dearly and is longing to forgive them—that He eagerly is waiting for their return. And so are we!

➤ Missing and inactive members: Best prospects for soul-winning

Some of the most effective soul-winning evangelists in our church have recognized that inactive Seventh-day Adventists can be the best prospects for becoming future leaders in our churches. Elder Fordyce Detamore considered missing members to be the most receptive people with whom he could work.

Here are some reasons we should not neglect missing members in our Witnessing Bible Study Program:

1. With their knowledge, they will have the most to give an account of in the Judgment Day.

2. They know, and most sincerely believe, the message of truth that we have to share with the world.

3. When truly converted, the inactive member will be one of the most enthusiastic and dedicated Christians in the church.

4. In most cases, these individuals will not be easily discouraged or need the care that a new convert without their background will need. They have been out in the old, cold world, and they know that it does not satisfy.

5. With very little instruction, the missing member can accept the whole message of salvation and in a short time be a powerful help to the cause of God.

➤ Fundamental principles for working with missing and inactive members

In working for those who have wandered away from the church, there are certain fundamental facts that we should understand:

1. Most of these people still believe that the Adventist Church has the truth for this day. Even though they are not living in accordance with God's standard, they have deep convictions concerning the correctness of our teachings in the major areas.

2. Most missing members do not want, nor do they need, lectures concerning the standards of the church. To tell them that they will die of lung cancer if they continue to smoke will only make them defensive and rebellious. By pointing out their sins, you focus their attention on their problems instead of pointing them to Christ, who is the solution to every one of their shortcomings. As a person dwells upon his sins and difficulties, they are magnified and seem insurmountable to him. As he looks to Christ, he gains courage and hope for the victory.

3. In order for the missing member to justify himself in the course of action he has taken that he knows is wrong, he will usually find fault with his parents, his church, or his fellow members. God has not appointed us to be a defense attorney for those the inactive member faults. When we attempt to correct the inactive member, we are aligning ourselves with an institution or individual that he feels has offended him. We, in effect, say, "We believe in these enemies of yours and not in you." Our job in working with these missing members is to win their friendship and confidence, not to argue with them or correct them.

4. Many of these individuals have something that they feel is

too great for God to forgive. They feel they have gone too far—that God is not willing to forgive and save them. This is not true, and we must be positive in our presentation of God's willingness to forgive and His desire to save. Make certain that your heart is filled with God's love so that you will have an abundant supply to share with the poor, wayward member who needs to find his way back to his Father's house.

5. The missing member often does not share his real feelings with you until he knows whether or not he can trust you. He may say and do things that are completely contrary to what he knows to be right. If you show your disapproval or appear to be shocked, he will take this reaction as a sign of your disapproval of him as a person. This will destroy your ability to help him in the future. When he tells you how bad he is or how he feels, tell him that in spite of his past God loves him and longs to prepare him a place in His eternal kingdom.

If you are a parent, you can compare your love and patience with your children to God's love and patience with each of His wayward children here on earth. And yet, God's patience and love is far greater than that of human parents.

➤ How to approach the missing or inactive member

Gain his confidence. Let him know that you would like to become his friend before you begin talking about his relationship to the Lord or to the church. This can be done by using the F-O-R-T method of visitation outlined on pages 21-23 of this manual.

1. As you let him talk about his family and his work, you will gain the right to ask him about his religious background. When you come to the R part of F-O-R-T, you might like to say to him, "I'd like to know something about your religious background." If he does not respond at once, you might add, "Were you raised a Seventh-day Adventist?" You will discover what has happened and why he is out of the church at the present time.

2. Instead of condemning or agreeing with the charges or excuses offered by the missing member, listen and be sympathetic to what he is saying. You must be neutral, because you do not know if what he is saying is fact or fantasy. You may wish to use two phrases that many have found helpful in response to criticism or bitterness. Say, "I'm sorry to hear that," or "That's too bad." This way you are not judging the person talking or defending the people he is criticizing.

   This will give you a friendly relationship to the offended one without his being able to say that you believe the same thing that he does about the church or the person who has offended him.

3. In most cases, the person out of the church, who still believes the message of the Adventist Church, will find excuses for his actions. He may not tell you on the first visit what the real reason is for leaving the church. If he is bitter or feels that the church or someone in the church has offended him, it'll help if you apologize on behalf of the church or its members. Say, "I'm so sorry to hear what has happened to you. As a member of the Seventh-day Adventist Church, I want to apologize to you for anything that I or any other Adventist has done that has discouraged you or caused you to feel as you do. Please forgive us, won't you?"

This will help lance the boil and remove much of the bitterness.

➤ Guidelines for visiting missing or inactive members

1. Pray at home or church for your prospect.

2. Study any information you have about the person. For example, why he was dropped from membership, his age, or his present interests.

3. Memorize the name and use it at the time of the visit.

4. Identify yourself and the church at the door. You should approach the prospect with warmth, tact, and gentleness.

5. Certain things to remember not to do when visiting missing or inactive members:

    a. Do not argue—you are a witness.

    b. Do not defend yourself, the church, or anyone else. You are not the defense attorney. Defending will only ally you with the hurt that person has experienced.

    c. Do not preach by telling the person that he should look to Jesus and not to other people.

6. The first visit may be short. If you are not acquainted, you may wish to use the F-O-R-T approach.

    a. "Good Morning! Is this where the Smiths live? Are you Mr. Smith? We are from the Adventist Church. We don't plan to stay long, but we do want to visit with you for just a little while. May we step in for a few minutes?"

(Use **F-O-R-T** here to get acquainted .)

F — Family
O — Occupation
R — Religious background
T — Testimony

b. "May I ask you a personal question? Do you still believe the Adventist message?" (If they say "Yes," then continue.)

c. "Have you thought recently about coming back to the church?" (If they say "Yes," rejoice with them and have prayer with them.)

Then invite them back and do anything you can to help them. If, on the other hand, they react negatively to questions "a" and "b," then be a good listener. Don't act shocked at what they may be doing or what they might say. Don't be defensive about the church. After they are through unburdening their heart, you might say, "Brother/ Sister, that's too bad. I'm so very sorry to hear that. I suppose that if I had been treated as you have been, that I would probably feel as badly as you do. From the bottom of my heart, I ask you to forgive us. One thing I am very sure about, and that is that God loves you."

Tell the person that the church does love him and invite him back.

Have prayer.

Missing or Inactive Member Survey

1. Were you raised in the Seventh-day Adventist Church?

   _____

2. How old were you when you joined? _____

3. Did you make your decision to join the church through a series of evangelistic meetings? _____

4. Were both your parents Seventh-day Adventists?
   Father _____ Mother _____

5. Did you receive any of your education in Seventh-day Adventist schools?

   Grade School   How many years _____
   High School   How many years_____
   College/University How many years_____

6. Did you marry a Seventh-day Adventist? _____

7. Did your marriage influence your church attendance?
   _____ If so, how?_____

8. How long did you attend church?

   _____

9. How long has it been since you have attended church regularly? _____

10. Do you still attend occasionally? _____

11. In which church did you last have your membership?

   _____

12. How long since you discontinued regular attendance at Sabbath School? _____

13. Did you feel that the regular study of the Sabbath School lesson was a help to you spiritually?_____
   If so, how? _____

14. When you discontinued regular church attendance, were you visited by anyone from the church? _____
   By whom?_____

15. What do you consider to be the chief reason you are no longer attending church?

   _____

16. Do you still believe the Seventh-day Adventist message to be God's truth for today?_____

17. Have you thought recently about coming back to the church?_____

18. Do you presently receive *Signs of the Times* magazine?

   _____

   To show our appreciation for your help in this survey, we would like to make you a gift of a year's subscription to *Signs of the Times.* Accepted offer? _____

   Name_____
   Address_____
   City _____ State_____Zip_____

   Surveyor's Name_____

Follow-up of Interests Created by Mass Media

(As presented by It Is Written *television. This approach can be adapted for any other media ministry follow-up.)*

1. Pray at home for your prospect.

2. Study the information you possess about the student: church affiliation, age, source of interests, etc. Prompt follow-up is necessary to assist in the making of right decisions at the time of conviction. Memorize his name and use it at the time of the visit.

3. Identify yourself and the program you represent at the door. You should approach the prospect with interest, warmth, tact, and gentleness.

4. Aim to build a bridge of understanding between yourself and the prospect. Be friendly, confident, relaxed. Smile— your new friend cannot relax if you are tense.

5. The first visit may be short. Here is a sample approach:

   a. "Hello. Is this where the Browns live? Are you Mr. Brown? We are from the It Is Written television program, Mr. Brown. We don't plan to stay, but we did want to inquire if you got the free offer you asked for?" (If the information indicates there has been a request.) If they have received the book, ask, "Have you had the opportunity to read the book?" If they have read the book, ask, "Did you enjoy it—and did you learn anything new?"

b. "Pastor Finley is interested in each viewer and would like to visit each person who responds to the program, if it were possible. But because this is not possible, he has asked us to visit you in his place. Often we find questions and problems that simply could not be handled by the mailman."

c. If they have finished a Bible course and show a good interest, ask, "Did you enjoy the course? Did you find the explanations to be in harmony with your understanding of the Bible?" If the answer is favorable, ask, "Would you be interested in studying the Bible further?" Or if the interest is good, give him an invitation to visit the church and invite him to be a dinner guest.

6. As a Christian, your sympathy, compassion and genuine interest in another person's well-being will soon be apparent. Your concern will guide you in what to say and how to act. You will not stay long—but your evident courtesy and consideration will prepare the way for your next visit.

7. "Have you heard about the special Bible study program that It Is Written is offering to all of its viewers?" If they say "no," explain the Bible program to them and then ask, "Would you like to take advantage of this special offer? I will be happy to leave the first two lessons and a Bible with you. Next week we will return at a time acceptable to you to see if you have any questions about the lessons or this special Bible study program."

8. Visits should be made regularly to deepen confidence that the Bible can help answer their daily problems and direct them to a new, fuller life. Only Christ-centered truth should be presented by the visitors, who have a genuine experience of conversion.

9. According to the degree of interest, invite to church, arrange for Bible studies, or enroll in additional course.

10. A short, fervent prayer may be offered in a standing or sitting position, if it is judged that to kneel may be embarrassing.

Principles for Gaining Decisions

*(Techniques and approaches,
compiled by R. Allan Anderson.)*

1. **Be Agreeable.** Discuss those features of truth on which you can agree.

   "If the worker keeps his heart uplifted in prayer, God will help him to speak the right word at the right time." —*Gospel Workers,* p. 120.

   "Agree with the people on every point where you can consistently do so."—*Evangelism,* p. 141.

2. **Be Alert.** Watch for indications that reveal the trend of the thoughts. Help the individual to build up his own conclusions. Remember that you are building a bridge, so drive down one timber at a time.

   "The sacred responsibility rests upon the minister to watch for souls as one that must give an account. He must interest himself in the souls for whom he labors, finding out all that perplexes and troubles them and hinders them from walking in the light of the truth."—*Gospel Workers,* pp. 190, 191.

3. **Be Direct.** Move straight on to your objective. Avoid any circumlocution. Keep the person's thought progression toward the goal. But do not go too fast.

   "The secret of our success and power as a people advocating advanced truth will be found in making direct personal appeals to the interested."— Ellen G. White, *Review and Herald,* August 30, 1892.

"Many times minds are impressed with tenfold more force by personal appeals than by any other kind of labor." —Ellen G. White, Letter 95, 1896.

4. **Be Kind and Courteous.** Remember that Jesus was always courteous. He never spoke an unkind word. Every morning He was given the tongue of the learned (Isa. 50:4).

    "He knew 'how to speak a word in season to him that is weary'; for grace was poured upon His lips, that He might convey to men in the most attractive way the treasures of truth."—*The Desire of Ages,* p. 254.

    "Into what you say, put the spirit and life of Christ." —*Evangelism,* p. 175.

    "Put all the Christ-like tenderness and love possible into the voice."—*Evangelism,* p. 174.

5. **Never Argue.** It is possible to win the argument and lose the man. A good salesman never argues. And the evangelist must be a good salesman.

    "Satan is constantly seeking to produce affronts by rude, acrid, violent thrusts; but Jesus found access to minds by the pathway of their most familiar associations. He disturbed as little as possible their accustomed train of thought."—*Evangelism,* p. 140.

6. **Make Abundant Use of Scripture.** Jesus met arguments of the Pharisees, and the temptations of the devil, by quoting from the Word of God. To every fresh challenge, He could reply, "It is written." And we will find our strength where the Saviour found His.

"Objections can each be met with a 'Thus saith the Lord.'"
—Ellen G. White, Letter 95, 1896.

Bible stories form a wonderful basis for an appeal to the heart. When Rebekah faced her real decision, she was hearing the call of God on the one hand and feeling the natural pull of home on the other. It was a crisis in her life and not an easy decision to make. But at last, she bravely said "I will go." That decision put her in the royal line.

Follow the sequence used by the farmer.

1. Prepare the soil.

2. Add fertilizer and the seed.

3. Cultivate the soil.

4. God will then send the sunshine and the rain of the Holy Spirit.

5. Then comes the harvest. Don't try to pick green fruit!

➤ Secure a surrender

Secure a surrender to Christ before presenting doctrines and the testing truths. Ask the right questions at the right time.

"Bring them to the point to decide. Show them the importance of the truth; it is life or death. With becoming zeal pull souls out of the fire."—*Testimonies,* vol. 1, p. 152.

"Many are convicted of sin, and feel their need of a sin-pardoning Savior. . . . If words are not spoken at the right

moment, calling for decision from the weight of evidence presented, the convicted ones pass on without identifying themselves
with Christ, golden opportunity passes, and they have not yielded,
and they go farther away from the truth."—*Evangelism,* p. 283.

"Ye have not because ye ask not."
—James 4:2

The Science of Securing Decisions

*The science of securing decisions consists of
properly applying those divinely appointed
laws, or principles, that govern the action of
the mind and heart in responding to
the call of God for obedience.*

➤ A study of how the mind works

Every gospel worker needs to understand clearly how the human mind works in making a favorable decision. This is basic in securing decisions.

"In order to lead souls to Jesus there must be . . . a study of the human mind."—*Testimonies,* vol. 4, p. 67.

"There are great laws that govern the world of nature, and spiritual things are controlled by principles equally certain. The means for an end must be employed, if the desired results are to be attained."—*Testimonies,* vol. 9, p. 221.

➤ Knowledge, conviction, and desire lead to decisions

Decisions stem from the interplay of knowledge, conviction, and desire in a person's mind. This is true according to Scripture and science. When a person's knowledge, conviction, and desire in reference to a given subject reach a certain intensity, the mind moves into decision and action with regard to it.

Since knowledge, conviction, and desire lead to decision, the sermons, the Bible studies, and the personal talks, should be an artful interweaving of the factors of desire and conviction in respect to the given subject. This is needed for bringing about the requisite interplay of knowledge, conviction, and desire for acceptance, decision, and action.

As we analyze certain texts, we discover that some are especially designed to bring knowledge, others to bring conviction, and still others to bring desire. And often the same text has in it the elements of all three. We need to focus on these texts that will implant conviction and at the same time arouse desire for accepting and following God's great principles as we present them in our Bible studies to the student.

➤ The direct personal appeal

Effective personal work is based on an adherence to a cluster of God-ordained principles, or spiritual laws. One of the most important is the use of the direct, personal appeal in conjunction with knowledge and desire. It is the secret of success in dealing with the interested people.

"The secret of our success and power as a people advocating advanced truth will be found in making direct, personal appeals to those who are interested, having unwavering reliance upon the Most High."—Ellen G. White, *Review and Herald,* Aug. 30, 1892.

One of the best illustrations of the principles involved in this direct, personal appeal is Paul's appeal to Agrippa, as recorded in Acts 26:22-28.

1. Use of the Word—knowledge.

    He prepared the way for making the personal appeal by an effective use of the Word. His appeal was based on the teachings of the Scriptures. Acts 26:22, 23.

2. Personal experience, creating desire.

The appeal should be connected with, or grow out of the person's own experience and knowledge. Paul used his own testimony as to how he found Christ and what Christ was to him. What was the reaction to Paul's testimony?

"The whole company had listened spellbound to Paul's account of his wonderful experiences. The apostle was dwelling upon his favorite theme. None who heard him could doubt his sincerity."—*The Acts of the Apostles,* p. 437.

3. Appeal directed to Agrippa's convictions.

Paul directed his appeal to Agrippa's convictions, taking the form of a question. He designed to bring home to Agrippa a realization of his personal responsibility. "King Agrippa, believest thou the prophets?" Acts 26:27 (first part).

4. Bringing the mind to the desired conclusion.

Paul's appeal is concluded by expressing confidence that Agrippa will respond. ""I know that thou believest." Acts 26:27 (last part). It was an appeal at an opportune moment.

Was Agrippa moved?

"Deeply affected, Agrippa for the moment lost sight of his surroundings and the dignity of his position. Conscious only of the truths which he had heard, seeing only the humble prisoner standing before him as God's ambassador, he answered involuntarily, 'Almost thou persuaded me to be a Christian.'"—*The Acts of the Apostles,* p. 438.

Using Texts As Direct Personal Appeals

"We should use those texts that are best designed for securing the desired results. We are to become scientific workers in the matter of reaching people with the truth of God."
—*Testimonies,* vol. 4, p. 93.

"General invitations are given; but not enough definite and personal invitations. If more personal calls were made, more decided movements would be made to follow Christ."—Ellen G. White, *Review and Herald,* Aug. 15, 1899.

Examples of how certain texts can be used in direct personal appeals.

1. For a decision to become a Christian.

    I would like to have you notice what Jesus says to you in Revelation 3:20: "Behold, I stand at the door, and knock: if any man hear my voice, and open the door, I will come in to him, and will sup with him, and he with me." Jesus wants to come into your heart and make your life what it ought to be. You want Him to come into your heart and make your life what it ought to be. You want Him to do this, don't you? You are ready now to open the door and let Him in, aren't you?

    Texts for the desire to accept Christ: Isa. 1:18; Matt. 11:28; Heb. 7:25; Psa. 34:8; Rom. 5:1; John 1:12; 2 Cor. 5:21.

Texts for the conviction to accept Christ: Acts 16:30, 31; John 3:16; Isa. 53:6; Matt. 16:26; John 8:24; Acts 4:12.

2. For the decision to keep the Sabbath.

   Is your objective a decision for keeping the Sabbath? Then focus what you present from the Bible on implanting under God the conviction that the seventh day should be kept holy, and at the same time arouse a desire for doing it.

   Texts for the conviction to keep the Sabbath: Ex. 20:8-11; James 2:10; Luke 6:46; Matt. 15:9; 1 Pet. 2:21; Mark 2:27; 1 John 2:3, 4.

   Texts for the desire to keep the Sabbath: Heb. 5:9; John 15:14; Rev. 22:14; Isa. 48:18; 58:13, 14; Isa. 56:1-6; Eze. 20:12; Ps. 40:8.

   Example: When you think of how Jesus gave Himself for you on the cross, you can't help loving Him. I know that you love Jesus. Here in John 14:15, Jesus says to you, "If you love Me, keep My commandments." Now that you see that one of His commandments is to keep the seventh day of the week, or Saturday, you are going to start keeping it because you love Him, aren't you?

   Do you know what two qualities the Lord is looking for in you and me? Notice what He says in Isa. 1:19: "If ye be willing and obedient, ye shall eat the good of the land." You want to be willing and obedient, don't you? Since the Lord has made it plain to you that the seventh day is the only day He ever sanctified for you to keep, you are willing to begin to keep it, aren't you?

3. For the decision to unite with God's remnant.

The Bible foretold that in the last days the Lord will gather out a special people to keep His commandments. In Isa. 27:12, God declares: "He will gather them one by one." Don't you want to be one of those whom the Lord is gathering for His kingdom?

Texts for the decision to unite with God's remnant: Rev. 18:4; John 10:26, 27; 2 Cor. 8:12; Luke 14:33.

➤ Build on their responses

Watch for the opportunity to build on the responses and admissions of your student as you study from the Bible. We should endeavor to turn their admissions and acknowledgements into steps which will lead them into a decision. This is a case of utilizing the principle of bringing a person's mind to the desired conclusion, by building successively on his own responses and admissions, as you and he talk back and forth. Often as you are studying with a person, he will of his own accord state that the teaching is true—that it is right.

Example: He may say, "You folks have certainly got the Bible on your side for keeping the seventh day." This is your opportunity to reply, "I am glad you see the truth about the right day to keep. It's fine to know the real truth. And do you know what the Lord wants you to do next?" Then turn to Luke 11:28: "But he said, 'Yea rather, blessed are they that hear the Word of God, and keep it.'" Then say, "Notice that Jesus pronounces His blessing on those who hear His Word and keep it, or obey it. So now that you see that the seventh day is Christ's day, the next thing is to keep it for Jesus."

➤ Using illustrations

The Bible contains many illustrations, incidents, and narratives which can be made the basis for powerful direct appeals to interested people whose cases or situations are parallel to the experiences set forth in the Bible.

1. The Israelites crossing the Jordan (Joshua 3). Use this in relation to the person who is willing to begin to keep the Sabbath if God will open the way in his home or work.

2. The two builders (Luke 6:46-49). Use this in relation to those who admit that the Sabbath is right but make no move to keep it.

3. The prodigal (Luke 15). Use this in relation to the backslider who feels he has gone too far for the Lord to receive him back.

➤ Miscellaneous texts for certain situations

For not allowing family or friends to keep one from obeying present truth: Matt. 10:37, 39; Luke 12:51-53; Gal. 1:10; Eze. 14:20.

For encouragement in the trials one may have in coming to Christ: Acts 14:22; John 15:18-20; 1 Peter 4:12-16; Luke 6:22, 23; Isa. 41:10.

For full surrender: Luke 14:33; 2 Cor. 8:9; Num. 32:11, 12.

For those who are striving to overcome evil habits: Jude 24; 1 John 5:14; James 4:7; Phil. 4:13.

"In working for the victims of evil habits, instead of pointing them to the despair and ruin toward which they are hastening, turn their eyes to Jesus. Fix them upon the glories of the heavenly. This will do more for the saving of body and soul than will all the terrors of the grave when kept before the helpless and apparently hopeless."—*The Ministry of Healing,* pp. 62, 65.

Discovering Obstacles and Meeting Objections

➤ Discovering the obstacles or problems in acceptance

The human mind is so construed that it cannot make a decision to enter upon a given course of action so long as there are detracting factors actively operating in the person's mind against it. In working with interested people who are holding back from making a decision, we must be alert to discover what is hindering them from accepting God's Word and be prepared, as far as possible, to remove the obstacle.

1. Discover what the obstacle is.

    "The sacred responsibility rests upon the minister to watch for souls as one that must give an account. He must interest himself in the souls for whom he labors, finding out all that perplexes and troubles them and hinders them from walking in the light of the truth."—Ellen G. White, *Review and Herald,* Aug. 30, 1892.

    "The minister must know the nature of the difficulties in the minds of the people, that he may know how to give every man his portion of meat in due season."—Ellen G. White, Manuscript 4, 1893.

    a. If you do not know what is holding a person back from keeping the Sabbath, attending church, receiving baptism, etc., you can visit endlessly and never get a decision from the person to take his stand and unite with the family of God. You must find the obstacle and then find a way to help the student solve the problem or bring texts to bear upon his problems.

"Many a laborer fails in his work because he does not come close to those who most need his help. With the Bible in hand, he should seek in a courteous manner to learn the objections which exist in the minds of those who are beginning to inquire, 'What is truth?' Carefully and tenderly should he lead and educate them, as pupils in a school."—*Gospel Workers,* p. 190.

b. "Your success will not depend so much upon your knowledge and accomplishments, as upon your ability to find your way to the heart."—*Gospel Workers,* p. 193.

By coming close to your student and winning his confidence, he will feel safe in expressing his feelings and problems to you. Encourage a give-and-take Bible study. Listen to what the student is saying. Encourage him to express his opinions on the topic being studied.

Even if his ideas are preposterous, never ridicule, laugh, or put down the student. You might say, "I'm glad you expressed yourself." Or, "I know that God has the answer—let's just pray and ask God to help us find a solution." This puts you in a different light; it isn't you on one side and the prospect on the other. You are on his side, asking God for the answer.

c. If the student says he does not agree with some point of truth, you might say, "I'm glad you expressed yourself. Let's discuss whatever section you didn't quite agree with. Perhaps I can help you." NEVER ARGUE. You may win the argument, but lose an interest. Dwell on the affirmative, not the negative points.

"If the worker keeps his heart uplifted in prayer, God will help him to speak the right word at the right time."—*Gospel Workers,* p. 120 (see also John 14:26).

➤ Meeting objections

Our natural tendency is to meet an objection head-on and beat it down.

1. Never argue—dwell on the affirmative.

    "Often, as you seek to present the truth, opposition will be aroused; but if you seek to meet the opposition with argument you will only multiply it, and that you cannot afford to do. Hold to the affirmative. Angels of God are watching you, and they understand how to impress those whose opposition you refuse to meet with argument." —*Testimonies,* vol. 9, pp. 147, 148.

    We strengthen their arguments when we repeat what they say. Keep always to the affirmative. Don't repeat their objection; present the solution and uplift Christ. (See *Gospel Workers,* p. 358.) It is usually not best to fire back with proof texts.

    First, you could say something like this: "I'm glad you told me how you feel about this. This means something to you, and I believe the Lord has the answer. Let's ask Him to help us." Then just offer a short prayer asking God to give an answer to the problem. Then meet the problem or objection with texts, if appropriate, for a solution.

2. Meeting objections with texts.

    It isn't possible to know beforehand what particular objection, excuse, or hindrance to a decision you will have to meet with your student, but there are a few general, familiar ones that we can have in mind when studying with our student in regard to keeping the Sabbath and uniting with God's Church:

a. Employment.

"I'll lose my job."

"I can't support my family if I don't work on Saturday."

"I can't find another job."

TEXTS: Matt. 6:30-33; Psa. 37:3, 25; Isa. 65:13, 14; Isa. 1:19, 20.

(Actual personal testimony is also good to use here.)

b. Business.

"Saturday is my best day for business."

"My business will be ruined if I close Saturdays."

"I'm in debt; I need all the money I can make."

"I'll never get ahead in the business world."

TEXTS: Matt. 16:26; Psa. 37:16; Mark 16:8; Mark 8:35; John 6:27; Isa. 56:2-5; Luke 12:19, 20. (Personal experience always helpful.)

c. Unpopular day to keep.

"It's so inconvenient to keep a different day."

"I'll be out of step with the rest of the world."

"So few keep Saturday—the majority keep Sunday."

"I'll lose my friends."

"People will ridicule me if I keep Saturday."

"I'll lose my social standing—they'll think I'm a fanatic."

TEXTS: Gal. 1:10; John 15:14; Luke 6:22, 23, 26; Prov. 29:25; Phil. 3:8; Matt. 10:37; John 15:19. (Personal testimony.)

d. Miscellaneous objections to Sabbath keeping.

"My pastor and friends advise me against doing it."

TEXTS: Isa. 8:20; 2 Kings 13:1-26; Acts 4:19.

"If it's right, why don't other great ministers and learned people keep it?"

TEXTS: 1 Cor. 11:1; 1 Cor. 1:26-29; Matt. 11:25.

"My mother and father kept Sunday. Why can't I be saved by doing the same?"

TEXTS: John 9:41; Eze. 18:20; Rom. 14:12; John 21:22.

"Sunday seems right to me."

TEXT: Prov. 16:25.

"I have a transportation job and work has to go on every day."

TEXT: Ex. 34:21.

"God doesn't care which day I keep, so long as I keep one in seven."

TEXTS: Ex. 20:8-11; Rom. 6:16; Lev. 10:1, 2; Deut. 4:2.

"God is so merciful, He'll save me if I do the best I can in keeping Sunday."

TEXTS: Gen. 4:1-7; James 4:17; Heb. 10:26; 1 Sam. 15:22.

(For most other questions as to which is the seventh day today, the calendar, etc., see notes and lesson answers in lesson #12 of the *In His Word* lessons.)

3. Meeting hindrances in a decision to unite with the Adventist Church.

   a. Cutting old ties.

   "I can't leave my church."

   "I promised my husband to stay in his church."

   "I intend to keep the Sabbath and stay in my own church."

   "Surely, God will not reject me if I stay in my church."

   TEXTS: Rev. 18:4; John 10:26, 27; 12;42, 43; Acts 4:19; John 1:35-40.

   b. Family opposition.

"My husband will leave me."

"If I join, my decision will bring division and discord into my home."

"My relatives will disown me."

"My children are bitterly opposed."

TEXTS: Psa. 27:10; Matt. 10:36, 37; Gal. 1:10; Luke 14:25-27; Isa. 41:10; Mark 10:29, 30.

c. Too much to give up.

"You require too much of people in your church."

"I can't give up . . . (smoking, dancing, coffee, pork, etc.)."

TEXTS: 2 Cor. 8:9; Matt. 13:45, 46; Luke 14:33; 1 John 5:4; Phil 4:13; 2 Cor. 5:17.

d. A more convenient time.

"I intend to do it later."

"In another six months my pension will come through."

"I'll feel better in a few months."

"I want to wait for my husband."

"I'm too old to change my ways now."

"I want to wait until the Spirit moves me."

TEXTS: Prov. 27:1; 2 Cor. 6:2; Heb. 4:7; 3:13; Isa. 55:6; Gen. 6:3; Psa. 18:44; 119:60; Matt. 25:1-13.

e. "It doesn't really matter."

"Joining a church will not save me anyway."

TEXT: Acts 2:47.

Since these excuses, misconceptions, or hindrances are so common, it is good to have them in mind when asking for decisions involving these topics. Ask the Holy Spirit to impress upon your mind just the right text to use. Be extremely gentle and loving in your manner of meeting objections or excuses. If you feel you have not been able to help your student, ask your pastor to give you help.

Christ's Method of Witnessing and Training

➤ **Christ's method alone will give true success in reaching people**

1. We want to use His method so it will guarantee success.

    a. Christ did not spend all of His time at large meetings preaching to the people. He more often went from house to house and met with one person at a time.

    b. He also used the personal contacts to gain the confidence of the people so that He could show them the way to the kingdom. For instance:

    • He associated with people as one who desired their good.

    • He showed His sympathy for them.

    • He ministered to their needs.

    • He won their confidence.

    • He then asked them to follow Him.

2. Wherever you see Jesus during His public ministry, you find Him talking to others about the kingdom.

    a. The Samaritan woman at the well (see John 4).

b. Nicodemus, the Jewish leader, at night (see John 3).

c. Simon, the Pharisee, at the feast (see John 12).

3. He did most of his soul winning one on one, leaving us a perfect example to follow.

➤ Christ used the in-service method of training the disciples for their work

1. He told a group of fishermen that if they would follow Him, He would teach them how to fish for human beings.

2. He also taught them by doing ministry before their very eyes. Again and again, they got to see the greatest soul winner of all time at work.

3. Then He sent them out two by two to practice what He had taught them.

4. When they returned and reported their problems, He told them how to do things better next time. We should use the same methods Jesus used to train the first disciples.

   • First, teach them the theory.

   • Second, teach them the truth as it is in Jesus.

   • Third, let them work alongside an experienced person in on-the-job training.

"They had listened to His discourses, they had walked and talked with the Son of God, and from His daily instruction they had learned how to work for the elevation of humanity . . .

"They taught what they had learned of Jesus, and were every day obtaining a rich experience. But they needed also experience in laboring alone. They were still in need of much instruction, great patience and tenderness. Now while He was with them to point out their errors, and counsel and correct them, the Savior sent them forth as His representatives."—The Desire of Ages, p. 340.

Jesus' example was far more effective than His instruction. Later, when He was no longer with them, every look and tone and word came back to them. And when conflicts came, they repeated His words and rejoiced at the success that came from emulating Him.

He sent the disciples out two by two, never alone. This way they could help and encourage each other, with each one's strength supplementing the other's weakness. We need to do our evangelism the same way today. Our ministers should educate the lay people instead of doing all the work themselves.